# Go The Extra Mile

## With Strong Middle Fingers

# Best
## of the Worst

# Pickiest Orders

# Smallest Tips

# Dumbest Customers

---

---

---

---

---

---

---

---

---

---

---

---

---

www.ingramcontent.com/pod-product-compliance
Lightning Source LLC
Chambersburg PA
CBHW071212220526
45468CB00002B/579